Irish Wolfhound
of the Past

Julie Hughes

Best Wishes
Julie Hughes
August 2013

ISBN 978-0-9552109-8-3

First published in Great Britain in 2010 by Julie Hughes

Printed and bound by
Martins the Printers Limited
Seaview Works, Spittal
Berwick-upon-Tweed, TD15 1RS
www.martins-the-printers.com

Set in 11/16 ITC Stone Serif and 10.5/14.5 ITC Stone Sans
Design by www.simprimstudio.com

Dedicated to my husband Brian
for his long suffering patience and humour

Introduction

I have lived with Irish Wolfhounds for over fourteen years, but it wasn't until about 8 years ago that I became so interested in their history.

We are very fortunate in the wolfhound world in that we have a few dedicated owners who do serious research into Irish Wolfhound pedigrees. Some of whom so kindly share their information.

I was fascinated by who owned these wonderful hounds in by gone days. I wrote a few articles for Irish Wolfhound breed magazines. I was encouraged to put these articles into "one place" and this little book is the result.

I am very grateful for the enormous assistance and kind help I have received throughout the last few years in researching "my companions".

I hope all enjoy reading what I have discovered, the photographs many from private family albums, will be of particular interest.

Julie Hughes
July 2010

Acknowledgements

For their kind help much appreciation must go to the following:

Anne Janis

Jeanne Patterson

Lois J Thomasson

Billie Hubner

Hilary Jupp

Gill Griffin

Sibley Historic Site, Minesota Museum, USA

Schloss Schonbrunn, Vienna, Austria

Royal Palace Godollo, Hungary

Steyning Museum

Mrs. Pat Dendy

Suzette Hill

Lord Adrian Palmer of Manderston

Dr. Hugh Wirth

Maisie Vince

Michael Galvin

Winchelsea Historical Society

Mary Dalgarno

Sally Stasytis

Mary Fitzpatrick

Anne Dammarell

S.P.C.A. Of Maryland, USA

Library of Congress

Photographs pp 112-113 copyright Hearst Corporation

Contents

Portrait of Henry Hastings Sibley as a young man.

1 Henry Hastings Sibley

IT WAS A POSTCARD that brought this gentleman to my attention. Henry Hastings Sibley was a fur trader, a politician and a military general, but above all he was a passionate hunter. He was born February 20th, 1811, in Detroit, he was descended from very early settlers who left England in 1629. After studying law at his father's law office, Sibley became Supply-Purchasing agent for the American Fur Trading Company. He was so successful, that despite his young age, he became a partner in that large influential company in 1834, just 23 years old. It was about this time that he moved to St. Peter's now Mendota, a sparsely populated area near the mouths of the Minnesota and Mississippi rivers. On the other side of the rivers to Mendota was Fort Snelling, a military outpost. This was pioneer country, wild and heavily forested. Minnesota was not to be made a state until later that decade.

In 1836 Sibley built the first stone house in the entire territory. Described as having the character of a hunting lodge, it still stands today. This house became a haven for all who passed; adventurers explorers, fur traders, missionaries, native Indians and of course, other hunters. Despite its remoteness, the house was said to be comfortable and quite large and all were made welcome. Sibley also had 6 horses and 12 "pedigreed" dogs.

In 1838 Sibley acquired from a Captain Martin Scott, a pair of rare Irish Wolfhounds, I wish it could be discovered from whose breeding, Lord Colonsay comes to mind, as someone who was alive at that time and breeding larger hounds. The pair were Lion and Boston, mistakenly sometimes called Tiger. Sadly, Boston was so ferocious, even against Sibley, that he had to be destroyed.

Lion became Sibley's constant companion, especially on the frequent hunts and the favourite amongst all the dogs. Sibley had built within the enclosure of his house, a lookout about 15 feet high. Around it's platform the railing was usually bordered with the heads of dogs resting on their paws, looking out over the prairie, probably reconnoitring for wolves. Lion though, had free run of the whole house and property. According to the adventurer and explorer, John Charles Fremont, Lion *". . . was companionable and had an affectionate disposition, and almost human intelligence."*

Pen portrait of Sarah Jane Sibley by a Mrs Eilet.

Life for the dogs and Lion went very well, as long as Sibley remained a bachelor. Sibley then met Sarah Steele, but as Freemont continues *". . . on the marriage of Mr. Sibley, May 1st 1843, Lion so far resented the loss of his first place that he left the house and swam across the Mississippi, to a fort (Snelling) where he ended his days."*

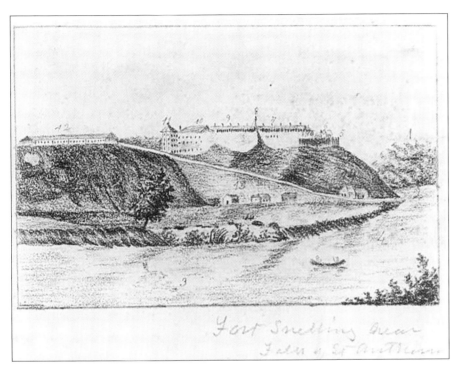

Fort Snelling circa 1840 Minnesota

Two views of Sibley's stone built home.

Lion was always glad to meet his master on his frequent visits over to the fort, keeping close by him and following him to the shore, though all persuasions failed to make Lion recross the river to the home where he had been supplanted.

In 1841 Sibley had commissioned a travelling artist, Charles Deas, to paint a life-sized portrait of his most beloved hunting companion. The portrait is exceptional, not only for its scale and subject matter for those days, but also because there are relatively few of Deas' paintings existing today.

When Lion died in 1847 Sibley himself wrote:

"My noble Lion! Fleet, staunch, brave and powerful.
Your master will never look upon your like again.
Old age and hard service have done their work upon you.
And the hunting grounds which knew you, shall know you no more"

The life sized portrait of Lion still hangs over the fireplace in Sibley's library in Sibley House.

Sibley went on to become Minnesota's first governor and later a Brigadier General. He died after a long illness on February 8th, 1891.

Life sized Portrait of Lion, beloved Irish Wolfhound of Henry Hastings Sibley. Painted by Charles Deas.

Engraved by G. J. Stodart from a photograph by J. Mayall.

Portrait of Lord Alfred Tennyson from a photo by J. Mayell.

2 Lord Alfred Tennyson

L ORD ALFRED TENNYSON was born in 1809 and died in 1892 and was of course, made Poet Laureate in 1850, appointed by Queen Victoria. There are many many biographies of Lord Tennyson out there, alas there is very little information about him and his dogs – apparently he had several during his life.

For us in the wolfhound world it is the hound Karenina that interests us. It has been rather a difficult research project and a great deal of the information on my part seems either "logical" or supposition.

What is known is that Karenina was one of eleven puppies in a litter born to Captain Augustus Graham's Banshee, an Irish wolfhound (whelped 1886, Sire: Bhoroo, Dam Hecla) and Mr. M K Angelo's leased male Borzoi Korotai. (Sire: Ataman Swerkai, Dam Pobarda) around the year 1888.

How did Tennyson enter our wolfhound world, because enter he did? We all know Captain Graham's huge influence on the resuscitation of our breed, perhaps a little less well known is Mr. Angelo's great help in this endeavour.

Karenina was a most beloved companion to Lord Tennyson and if he hadn't been one of the most foremost literary figures of the Victorian age, we would not ever have heard of her.

It should be a reminder that Captain Graham, like many of the great influences in the Irish Wolfhound breed, was firstly a deerhound breeder, as was Richardson, Angelo, Colonsay and the few others so interested in wolfhounds.

Sidney Dobell, also a renowned a poet of the time, lived at Cricket Hall in Gloucestershire. Captain Graham lived at Rednock in Gloucestershire. It would be very surprising if they did not know each other with their common hound pursuits. Remembering that in those days the hound world was even smaller than today. It is said that one of Sidney Dobell's deerhounds was the model leaning against the vacant chair in the much loved portrait of "The Empty Chair" by Briton Riviere.

It is not such a leap of the imagination to suppose that Lord Tennyson acquired Karenina through the introduction from Dobell to Captain Graham and acquiring one of the 11 puppies from Banshee and Korotai.

Three Borzois by Maud Earl, Karotai in the foreground.

Tennyson Sculpture by George Frederick Watts OM, RA. In front of Lincoln Cathedral.

Lord Tennyson died in 1892 at the age of 83, Karenina, his beloved hound was still probably alive, although, I have no certain confirmation of this.

A long time friend and sculptor was George Frederick Watts, he was commissioned by the good burghers of Lincoln, Tennyson's birthplace to erect a monument to Lord Tennyson. The original statue was to have Lord Tennyson in a toga! Many were horrified at this idea and Watts wanted a more realistic representation, hence the statue that stands in Lincoln Cathedral Close today. Watts knew that Karenina was a very beloved companion to Tennyson, hence the inclusion of the hound. Watts, though wasn't used to sculpting dogs and so wrote to Briton Riviere for advice. Riviere had, as mentioned, painted hounds many times before and was also married to Sidney Dobell's sister Mary Alice Dobell – again what a small world. The monument was erected in 1905 and what a beautiful thing it is.

This not the last mention of Karenina by any means. In 1899, seven years after Tennyson's death Brition Riviere exhibited at the Royal

Acadamy, the following portrait of Lady Tennyson.

Many, understandably confuse this portrait as being of Lord Tennyson's wife, but no it is of his daughter in law, Audrey the 2nd Lady Tennyson, married to Lord Tennyson's eldest son Hallam. Lord Alfred Tennyson's wife was Emily Sellwood.

As mentioned earlier, I have no idea if Karenina was still alive when this portrait was painted but to be exhibited at the Royal Acadamy it had to be a "new" work of art and the year was 1899. So I can only assume that Brition Riviere did the painting from memory or the younger Tennysons "inherited" her. This is entirely possible as Lord Hallam was also very fond of dogs. Brition Riviere also painted Lord Hallam with a tall bloodhound type dog.

Both portraits are now actually the property of the National Library of Australia. Lord Hallam Tennyson became governor of South Australia in 1899 and was obviously fond enough of both portraits to take them with him.

There are couple of very obscure references to Lord Tennyson having had a previous hound amongst his ownership of several dogs. Lufra, was apparently a steel grey hound, perhaps a deerhound, perhaps from Sidney Dobell? The hound in the sketch "Tennyson in his Library" does not look a bit like Karenina, could this be the elusive hound Lufra? I think so! One reference from a visiting poet to Tennyson 's home quotes:-

"... we walked Tennyson and I with hounds Lufra and Karenina in peaceable quietude."

Lady Audrey Tennyson with Karotai by Briton Riviere. National Library of Australia.

Sketch: Tennyson in his Library

I am not a big poetry fan and did not realise that the following words were written by Tennyson:-

I hold it true, whate' er befall
I feel it, when sorrow most,
"Tis better to have and lost
than never to have loved at all"

I think many wolfhound companions have thought of the last two lines at times!

1869. L'Imperatrice Elisabetta d'Austria.

3 Empress Elizabeth of Austria and Hungary

ELIZABETH WAS BORN IN 1838, the daughter of a Bavarian Duke. Called Sissi by friends and family, she was very fortunate that growing up in the family castle in Bavaria, her childhood was carefree and relaxed with horses, dogs and freedom.

That all changed when at the age of 15 she met Franz Joseph Hapsberg who was to become Emperor of the Austrian Empire. Married at 16 in 1854, Elizabeth was shocked and dismayed by the strict and rigid etiquette of the Austrian Court. The court was equally surprised and appalled at the beautiful but wayward young country girl who would in time become their Empress.

Elizabeth certainly was beautiful! Her hair was so long it almost reached the ground, and her figure was perfect, with a lovely face. She was very aware of how she looked and spent a great deal of time exercising and lived on strange diets, often detrimental to her health. She also took baths with milk for her complexion. Interestingly, she hated her teeth which she thought too yellow, so rarely spoke in public and tended to mumble at social functions.

The court was ruled by the Archduchess Sophia, Franz Joseph's mother and a very formidable powerful woman. She planned from the time of her son's marriage to Elizabeth to be in charge of all aspects of the young couple's lives. Sophia made Elizabeth's life a misery. Even her children were whisked away to be brought up under the influence of the Archduchess.

Elizabeth rebelled and escaped from the pressures of court life by travelling and hunting. She was a much admired and accomplished horsewoman and she hunted all over the main land and islands of Europe. The speed and danger of fox or stag hunting exhilarated her, although, she refused to be in on "the kill".

Elizabeth had several dogs during her life, including, it is said, seven Leonbergers, a gift from Germany, also a Great Dane and a Borzoi. She was always surrounded by several "toy" varieties of dogs. It seems though, that it was the Irish Wolfhound Shadow that captured her heart.

It was in the mid 1860s that Shadow was given to Elizabeth as a puppy. It has been said that Shadow came from a kennel in Dublin,

From a full length portrait of Elizabeth at aged 27 by Franz Xaver Winterhalter.

Franz Joseph Hapsberg and Elizabeth the year of their marriage 1854.

Elizabeth with a young Shadow.

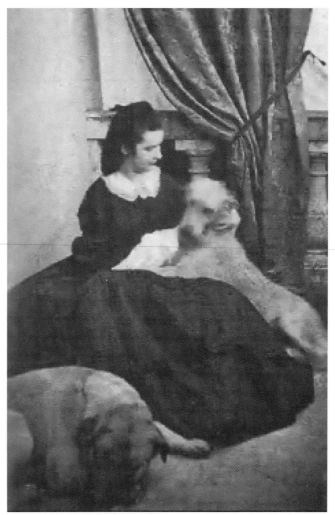

Kaiserin Elisabeth

Elizabeth and Shadow in Schobrunn.

Sketch from the Museum Schonbrunn.

Shadow's grave in the gardens of the Royal Palace
Godollo.

and also suggested that he had the"look" of one
bred by Lord Caledon, although this could not
be confirmed.

Elizabeth did not visit England or Ireland until
1874.

Elizabeth travelled a great deal, and Shadow
was her constant companion everywhere she
went. When in Hungary, then part of the Austrian
Empire, her favourite home was Godollo Castle,
just outside of Budapest.

Sadly, it was at Godollo Castle that Shadow
died in 1875 from dysentery. Elizabeth was grief
stricken, so upset was she, that she could not
attend the wedding of her younger brother. Franz
Joseph immediately sent for another wolfhound
from apparently the same elusive Irish kennel.
Mohammed though, never could replace Shadow
in her affections. Shadow was buried at Godollo
Castle where his grave can be seen to this day.

A statue was also placed of Elizabeth and
Shadow in the beautiful gardens at the castle.

Elizabeth may have had a difficult time at
the cold and humourless Austrian court but the
people of Austria and Hungary adored her, her

beauty and her spirit. Also, a sad life in many ways, despite her position. She lost her son Rudolf in the "Mayerling" catastrophe, her beloved sister perished in a dreadful fire in Paris and members of her family had a tendency to insanity. Elizabeth herself was murdered by a crazed anarchist in September 1898, she was just 59. She was mourned by all of Europe, but the photos of her and her Shadow seem to me, to be the most moving.

Statue of Elizabeth and Shadow in the gardens of the Royal Palace Godollo.

Porcelain image of Shadow c 1870's.

Thomas Bolton around 1894 outside his veterinary surgery with Vandal and Nell.

4 Thomas Bolton

MANY OF US, IN THE IRISH WOLFHOUND WORLD are familiar with the photograph of Thomas Bolton standing outside his veterinary surgery with two wolfhounds in about 1894, the two wolfhounds being Vandal and Nell. The photograph is in Captain Graham's Pedigree book and other well read Irish wolfhound books. I have always thought the gentleman looked rather forlorn. Naturally, the photograph is misleading:

Thomas Henry Bolton was born in 1862. His father, also named Thomas Henry Bolton was a Member of Parliament for the Liberal Party and they lived at Burwash Estate near Heathfield, Middlesex.

Bolton trained as a veterinary surgeon and set up his practice in 1893 in Steyning, a small town near Brighton. He had married Eva, a lady from Eastbourne, in Sussex in 1890. Together they bought No.33 and No.35 Church Street, in Steyning. No.35 was pulled down and a larger three storey house was built from where the veterinary surgery operated.

The pair had eight children; seven boys and one girl: Tom, John, Herbert, Robert, Frederick, Edwin, Felix, Charles and Anne. The children and servants lived in the small cottage of No.33, whilst their parents lived above the surgery, sounds like a rather good arrangement.

It is entirely possible that Bolton first started in hounds with deerhounds as his contemporaries and friends Captain Graham and M.K.Angelo did. Although, this would have been in the 1880s and Bolton therefore, would have been just in his twenties.

Captain Graham outside his home Rednock Glos.

It is thought that Bolton's first Irish wolfhound was Ballymena born 30th March, 1896, bred by Angelo out of Goth II and Brenda. This girl did belong at first to a Mr. C. Lee Roberts, who lived in Oxford. Interestingly, Graham makes a particular reference to Thomas Bolton with regards to Angelo's Oscar, saying "Bolton knew this dog well". Oscar being the litter brother to Brenda, the dam of Ballymena.

In the photograph, the hound lying down is the bitch Vandal, born in 1892, who also belonged to Angelo, and from whom he had three litters – Angelo sold or gave Vandal to Bolton, who bred one litter from her using Bran II as the sire. Graham describes Bran II as a very tall dog, 31 ½ inches, with good feet and legs. Angelo also bred Bran II who eventually went to a Mr. C Smith. Mr Smith apparently gave Bran II's stuffed head to Delphis Gardner!

Two puppies came from this litter; Doris and Tara, both girls went to the Hon. Miss E. Dillon, who had been in wolfhounds

Bran II

Steyning Wolf 1903

since at least 1892. Tara then went on to Major Richardson.

The other hound that is standing next to Bolton in the first photo was Nell, born in 1897, she was described as a red fawn, rather Borzoi-ish, 30½ inches tall. Nell was always known as Steyning Nell, and the first of Bolton's hounds to be know with this affix.

In the early 1900s few were that interested in the Irish wolfhound, but these few were passionate about the betterment of their beloved breed. This small collection of breeders bred their hounds together and the litters went to the same people over and over again.

The next litter that Thomas bred was 22nd May, 1899, once again Angelo's Bran II was the sire but this time he was put to Steyning Nell. Just the one puppy was registered, Prince Lucio, who went to Miss M. Kearn, a lady well known in this small wolfhound world.

Meanwhile, Bolton's veterinary practice was thriving and he earned the respect of farmers and villagers, area wide for the care of their animals. The Boltons were known as pillars of the community of Steyning. Bolton was a sides man at the local church, St Andrews, which stands just behind the surgery building. The family had their own pew – a much favoured mark of respect.

Thomas Bolton and his wife were rather successful in their lives, but not in the wealth league of Graham and Angelo, although it seems they remained close friends through the wolfhounds. Also, Bolton did not seem to have "kennels" as such. He didn't have as many hounds for one thing, as his two friends, who often had up to 20 hounds any one time. Bolton's hounds seemed to have lived with the family in their home. He also rented for over 40 years from the Goring estate, later buying it, a large field right next to the church and again right behind his surgery and house. This field was actually always called the "Bolton " field and where the hounds had "free run" exercise every day. Today this field is the home of Steyning Grammar School.

In 1902 Steyning Nell and Wolf 11 (again another of Angelo's hounds) were mated and 4 puppies were produced; Doris, Glengarrif, Steyning Mickey and Steyning Wolf.

An older Bolton in front of his field with the Church in the background.

Ch. Cloghan of Ouborough .

Halcyon Kennels' CH. STEYNING SORREL HALCYON

In 1902 Thomas seems to have acquired a Killybegs bitch which he bred to the famous O'Leary that belonged to Mr. Crisp. This produced just the one hound Zulu who went to a Mr. C. Worts.

Bolton's last litter at this time was using his own Doris (born 1902) and Brian Astore belonging to a Mrs Hall in February 1905. Again just the one puppy was registered:

Vandall 11. Interestingly, this Vandall was exported to the USA although, I could not find to whom she went.

It is of course, very possible that Bolton bred other litters in this early part of the twentieth century, but were not registered and that maybe he had more hounds around his home than we know.

I don't suppose we will ever really know why Bolton stopped breeding his wolfhounds in 1905. Steyning Micky, Steyning Wolf, Gengarrif and Doris could still have been alive up until 1910 or even later. One reason could have been the death of Captain Graham in 1909, so many breeders of this era considered Graham their mentor. More seriously I feel, for Thomas, was the death of Angelo in 1912. Also, remember Bolton's litters

Steyning Coleen

appeared to have been small, and perhaps this also disappointed him, although we have no idea if some of the pups were lost to disease.

In 1914 though, world events stopped virtually all breeding of dogs in the UK. It is hard to imagine the devastation that World War 1 brought to the dog world. Thousands of dogs were put down, because of lack of food. If one dared to have a litter of any kind, it could not be easily registered, and if not registered did not really exist.

For Thomas Bolton, World War I was particularly hard, and I am sure Irish Wolfhounds were the last subject on his mind at the time.

Of Bolton's seven sons, five joined the army (Frederick and Felix Charles were too young).Tom the eldest son, had actually gone to Canada to farm, in 1911. On the outbreak of war he immediately joined the Canadian Mounted Rifles and returned to Europe. John and Robert Bolton both joined the Cavalry.

In 1916 sadly both Tom and John were killed in action, more tragic still, Robert had the awful experience of seeing John being killed by the mortar shell that hit him. Both Tom and John died gallant deaths and were posthumously awarded Victory Medals the British War Medal plus the 1914-15 Star.

The remaining sons, Herbert, Edwin and Robert did return unharmed from the battle fronts. Herbert then chose to assist his father for the next many years in the practice, although it is not certain if he qualified as a veterinary surgeon. Robert did very well on the railways and was awarded a medal by the Queen. Frederick and Felix Charles became bus drivers and Edward was a taxi driver. Anne, Bolton's only daughter studied at the Royal College of Music, before marrying and having twins.

In the 1926 Irish Wolfhound Club year book, Thomas Bolton is in the list of members. Bolton is now in his 60s, Herbert is helping him with his successful veterinary practice, the children are all grown up and there are grandchildren around and close by. Bolton re-entered the Irish Wolfhound world with vigour. He acquired Broadbridge Brenda from a Mrs. S. H Whalley. The name "Broadbridge" was presumably taken from the small town where Mrs. Whalley lived. Kennel affixes were still in their infancy (today place names are not permitted). Brenda was either sold or given by Mrs. Whalley but was actually bred by Mr. R. Montague Scott of the famous Ifold kennels, her sire being Patrick of Ifold and her dam Angelina of Ifold. She was born June 1925.

As you will see below, Brenda was very important to Bolton's breeding program. Her first litter was on 13th February 1927 to Cromac owned by Mr. Isaac Everett. He was out of Felixtowe Chreeshe by Felixtowe Conbec, born 4th October 1922.

This litter produced: Felixstowe Kisheelen, Steyning Norah, Steyning Shielah and Felisxtowe Kilfree Halcyon who was exported to the United States.

This mating was repeated and on 23rd November 1927 produced Bournstream Peter and Felixstowe Kilsaran, both were exported to the United States and Felixstowe Paddy.

One can see that Bolton was now involved with the famous kennel names that we are familiar with today. Particularly noticeable in the following litters:

Fergus of Ouborough x Broadbridge Brenda – 20th August 1928 whelping Eileen of Ouborough, Mick of Ouborough and Steyning Doris.

Sulhamstead Demon x Broadbridge Brenda – 25th July 1929 with just one puppy registered; Bwana O'Meagher of Lumbwa.

Chulainn Connacht x Steyning Shielah – 15th August 1929 whelping Banshee Nan, Bournstream Brian, who was exported to the United States, Paddy Next Best Thing, Steyning Coleen, Steyning Dermot, Dorema of Contaria and Staly Vandal.

The Chulainn Copper x Broadbridge Brenda – 2nd September 1930, produced a larger litter, Buster Boy, Iomar of Ouborough, Moltarna, Shaugh of Cuckmere, Steyning Lisa and Steyning Sorrell of Halcyon.

That same year, 1931 Cloghan of Ouborough was mated to Steyning Shielah producing Dreumah of Ouborough.

Bolton's last litter was March 16th 1935, this time mating his Steyning Lisa to the famous Rippingdon Dan of Southwick resulting in a litter of eight; Bana of Brabyns, Barley Suga, Ealga of Brabyns, Patricia of Graedlea,

Steyning Shawn, Steyning Starling (who was exported to the United States) and Steyning Elmo, whose name was changed to Gui of Pentavalon and exported to Canada.

Broadbridge Brenda was very highly thought of by Bolton. Breeding her five times was not unusual in those days and Brenda was the "big pet" of the family, the whole family including the grandchildren loved her. When Bolton's youngest son Felix Charles had his second daughter she was named Brenda in honour of the favourite hound, Broadbridge Brenda.

Herbert Bolton not only assisted Bolton in the veterinary practice but also became a member of the Irish Wolfhound Club, and Steyning Doris was registered in his name, although she was later transferred to a Mrs. D. A. Brooks.

Steyning Sorrell was exported to Mrs Clark of the Halcyon kennels where she was always known as Steyning Sorrell of Halcyon and became a United States Champion and an important part of that kennel's breeding programme. Steyning Coleen stayed with Thomas and was shown.

As mentioned earlier, in the Bolton household the hounds were very much treated as members of the family; another of the hounds that stayed with Bolton was Paddy Next Best Thing, a grandson of Broadbridge Brenda. I am indebted to Mrs Patricia Dendy for these photos. Mrs Dendy is the granddaughter of Thomas Bolton, her father being Felix Charles. The photographs show Mrs Dendy as a baby, Anne her Aunt and Eva, Bolton's wife and Paddy. Also,

Mrs Dendy as a baby, Anne and Eva, Bolton's wife and the hound Paddy.

Mrs Dendy as a little girl with again Anne and Paddy.

Bolton and his wife Eva in Bolton Field in the 1920s

Mrs. Dendy as a little girl with her mother Anne.

Issac Everett commented in one of his articles on Irish Wolfhounds of those days that "Thomas Bolton was a real stayer" in the Irish Wolfhound breed.

Eva Bolton died on January 1st 1942 aged just 70, sadly Bolton died just three weeks later at the age of 80. Both are buried at the church of St Andrews along with their sons, so close to their home. The photograph is a favourite of mine, although it does not include a wolfhound, it is such a happy photograph of Bolton and his wife Eva taken in the mid 1920s.

Hunting portrait of Sir Eric Palmer early 1940s

5 Sir Eric Palmer

I FIRST DISCOVERED THE NAME ERIC PALMER many years ago now, reading Ferelith Somerfield's excellent biography of Florence Nagle. I remember the few lines;

"Mr. Eric Palmer of Huntley and Palmer fame had a litter and Florence with the artist Cecil Aldin went to see the puppies. He bought a bitch puppy and Florence a dog puppy."

I vaguely wondered who this gentleman was, but gave no further thought to it until I came across his name again. I was given as a gift Heron's *Cecil Aldin, The Story of a Sporting Artist* and on page 153 "Cecil Aldin had been instrumental in obtaining for Mrs. Nagel her first wolfhound from Eric Palmer"

Goodness, I thought, why don't we know more about this person who gave Florence Nagle her very first wolfhound, thereby the beginning of what would become one of the best and certainly most famous Irish Wolfhound Kennels of the 20th century.

Many hours of research though, revealed very little, apart from the fact he was indeed a member of the large family of Palmers of the very well-known Huntley and Palmers biscuit manufacturers and that he was born in 1883.

Sometime later I was very kindly given the name of Sir Eric Palmer's great niece and direct descendant, Suzette Hill, by her cousin Lord Adrian Palmer of Manderston, Duns.

Suzette has been very generous in sharing with me details of Sir Eric Palmer's life and especially some wonderful private photographs.

Sir Eric Palmer was born in 1883, the eldest son of Charles and Ethel Palmer of Bozedon House, Oxfordshire. A brother Geoffrey and two sisters Clare and Vera were to follow.

The family were all keen horse riders and Charles Palmer and the two sons rode with the South Berkshire Hunt as often as possible. There were always dogs around the house of various breeds. It is thought that two dogs in the family portrait were long haired Manchester terriers.

Sir Eric's first wolfhound was bought from Samuel Kennedy. Hibernia was born 5th April 1907, out of Barney x Shelagh, also bred by Samuel Kennedy. In the 1926 annual year book of the Irish Wolfhound Club, Miss M.S. Kearns discusses "Parental influence on Type". She mentions Hibernia as quite a small wheaten bitch, but very beautiful. Hibernia did become an English Champion.

In 1910 Sir Eric married Gwen Jones, an Australian lady and an accomplished horse rider. They moved to Shinfield Grange in Berkshire. That same year Hibernia was bred to Aughrim (Ch.

The Charles Palmer Family: Sitting: Eric, Ethel, Geoffrey and standing Vera, Charles and Clare.

Wargrave whelped 1897 x Acushal whelped 1899) Aughrim was considered a very beautiful type with perhaps the most perfect head of his day.

This litter produced the huge Donegal. Quoting again from Miss Kearns in 1926 "perhaps the most beautiful wolfhound we have had, who stood 37 ½ inches and was a larger edition of his sire, not quite such a beautiful head but the same lovely quality. He died of distemper when only 16 months old, before he had attained his full development or lost his awkward puppy movement and nervousness.

Donegal raised a storm of jealous criticism, as all extra beautiful dogs do, and his detractors would not allow anything for his youth, I suppose because they knew that if he had lived he could beat anything they ever bred."

I believe that the photograph on p39 shows Donegal having a conversation with Sir Eric Palmer's baby daughter, Barbara Mary, showing the great temperament that we as lovers of the breed have come to cherish.

In 1913 Sir Eric bred Hibernia again, this time to Ch. Ivo Dennis another son of Aughrim's.

Hibernia

Aughrim

Family photo of Hibernia with Clare Palmer, Sir Eric's sister

Brian and Hibernia, in the grounds of Sir Eric's house Shinfield Grange with a nursemaid

Probably Donegal having a conversation with Sir Eric Palmer's baby daughter Barbara.

This breeding included Manin Michael, Biddy and Bran.

Manin Michael became Sir Michael of Sheppey and was bought by Florence Nagle, (then Watson), to become, as before mentioned, her first Irish Wolfhound. She paid £5.00 for him. Cecil Aldin the artist, bought Biddy, his sister for the same sum, Cecil Aldin and Sir Eric having been friends of long standing.

Sir Eric kept Brian, who was bred to Lady Alma of Sheppey owned by Florence Nagel. This produced the famous Sulhamstead Pedlar who can be found in many of our present day pedigrees. Also in 1912 Sir Eric and Cecil Aldin became joint Mastership of South Berks Hunt, a great pleasure for them both.

Sadly in 1914 the Great War began and Sir Eric enlisted with the army and this seems to have been the end of his personal involvement with Irish Wolfhounds. So many other breeders had to give up because of their role in the military and the food shortages, plus any litters born could not be easily registered during this time.

On his return to Reading after the war Sir Eric devoted his time to the family business

Michael and Biddy

Sir Eric Palmer in World War I

Huntley & Palmer, his family and hunting, probably now largely with the Garth Hunt in Berkshire. His friendship with Cecil Aldin resumed and continued until Aldin's death in 1935.

There are no records of Sir Eric belonging to the Irish Wolfhound Club, but along with his duties with the family firm, he did become the Editor of the widely acclaimed *The Field* magazine in 1930 and remained Editor until 1933. As Editor he purchased an advertisement in the Club year book 1930-1-2.

Around 1931 Sir Eric's wife Gwen and her sister in law Vera Palmer visited Camp da Mar in Majorca, home to Cecil Aldin. Micky, Cecil Aldin's wolfhound made famous by the artist's illustrations was still alive at that time. I mention this as I wanted show this family photograph of Gwen Palmer and probably Aldin's wife having a wonderful time with Cracker the bull terrier and it is possible that one of the dogs on the distant beach is Micky.

In 1933 Sir Eric became Chairman of Huntley & Palmer's Biscuits. When World War II broke out in 1939 he was in the forefront in the effort to get food to the troops. He worked tirelessly throughout the war and in 1946 he was awarded a Knighthood in the New Year's Honours List for Services to Industry. Sadly he died in 1948 aged just 65.

At his funeral the whole of Shinfield village turned out. The lanes were lined with jostling hounds, kennel lads and scarlet coated huntsmen, their bugles sounding a poignant but stirring note as the cortège passed by.

Although, Sir Eric Palmer's association with Irish Wolfhounds was just for a few years at the turn of the 20th century, I think he deserves a place in our history, as someone who had, without probably realising it, some influence on the future of our breed.

Gwenn Palmer and probably Aldin's wife at Camp da Mar in Majorca circa 1931

Mrs Evan Hunter with Mr. Rodolph, Robur Randy and
Fodhla Patrick. 1913

6 Mrs Evan Hunter

A S ONE CAN IMAGINE, interest in the Irish Wolfhound in the early twentieth century was rather minimal in Scotland, but coming across the following quote in the *Illustrated Kennel News* of December 15th 1916, I was intrigued.

"It is doubtful if the Irish Wolfhound has a truer and more generous friend than Mrs. Evan Hunter, but for whose efforts the interest in the breed in Scotland would certainly have died"

So who was Mrs Evan Hunter? Despite a great deal of searching in all the archives and records available, there is sadly very little known of this early Scottish fancier and companion to our beloved breed.

It seems that what ever few mentions of this lady there are in the chronicles of the day, she was always known as Mrs Evan Hunter: that just wasn't good enough.

Jane Ritchie Kay was born in 1891 to a good family of some social standing in Perth, moving some time later to 10 Ravelston Park, Edinburgh. On 1st August 1913 aged 22 Jane married Mr. Evan August Hunter.

A little more is known about Mr. Evan Hunter. At the time of the marriage, Mr. Hunter was a lawyer with his father's firm, Messrs E.A. & F. Hunter, the family firm being prestigious enough to belong to "The Writers to the Signet" a peculiar

Scottish Law Society enabling members special authority and prestige through work for the Royal Courts of old and a Royal voice of authority on behalf of the King.

Once married Jane and Evan Hunter moved to Evan's residence at 13 Heriot Row, a magnificent town house in what is called "new town Edinburgh" minutes from famous Princes Street and four stories high. This property is now a " Sleep Disorder Clinic".

How they met or why they married is not known, except they both seem to have had a interest in sport. Mr Evan Hunter's father was a rather well known Scottish Cricketer, and Evan himself was interested in running. Mrs Hunter, unusually, seems to have been an accomplished badminton player.

It seems in that first year of marriage that Mrs. Hunter threw herself in to the world of the Irish Wolfhound. Late in 1913 and early 1914 she acquired her wolfhounds taking the name Robur for her kennel affix.

Robur Rapture a bitch born July 27th 1913 out of Felixstowe Gelert and Lindly Lupin was her first. Followed by Mr. Rodolph, a son of Ivo O'Neil and a Ch. Garth bitch. Robur Randy was out of Felixstow Kilronan and Felixstowe Fiona . She then bought two dogs from a Mr. J. Mckelvie, Robur Rector and Fodhla Patrick born April 26, 1913 litter brothers out of Lindly Hector and Felixstowe Kilrush.

Mrs. Hunter started showing almost immediately and was seen as a great encouragement to the Irish Wolfhound fancy in

Mr. & Mrs. Evan Hunter with Fodhla Patrick. KC SB 181T. 1914

Scotland as she assisted with show committees, offering trophies and guaranteeing classes. Her hounds did very well, Fodhla Patrick in particular, at his first show, in Glasgow when just a puppy, he came overall second in a large open class. That same year 1914 he won three 1sts and the challenge certificate at the Irish Kennel Club Show in Dublin. Mr. Rodolph was a winner at the Scottish Kennel Club and other Scottish shows. Robur Randy was considered a truly good bitch of the time, winning at the Edinburgh Summer show, coming 3rd at the large Richmond show. Mrs. Hunter was very enthusiastic indeed.

Then war was declared and Mr Hunter was called to serve with the Scottish Horse, where he was given a commission. He actually was attached to the Royal Artillery Supply Corp. which meant a great deal of travelling and Mrs Hunter seemed to have travelled with him, some of the time. Sadly, 1914 was not kind to the new kennel Mrs. Hunter was trying to build, both the beautiful bitch Robur Rapture and Robur Rector, the litter brother to Fodhla Patrick died of distemper. Nevertheless, Mrs. Hunter expressed her desire to breed something really good and hoped that after the war, she could build up further, her involvement with the wolfhounds.

In February of 1915 Mr. Hunter was promoted to Captain. Dog shows were scarce particularly in the north of England and Scotland, but what few there were, Mrs Hunter attended. Many show executives were grateful indeed for her support and kindly actions. Her hopes were centred on the end of the war so as to breed and build up her Robur kennel, now only having the three remaining hounds. One must remember that few litters born during the war were registered. Fodhla Patrick continued to do very well at shows after his early successes, coming first in open and first in limit at Crufts in early 1916. He gained his second challenge certificate soon after Crufts at the Ladies Kennel Association, then at Manchester,his third, giving him what was considered his well deserved Championship. Many thought Pat as he was called at home should have received his honours sooner than the middle of 1916, but he was always up against the "elite" of the day in his breed.

At the end of 1916 Ch. Fodhla Patrick was fully developed, very tall and weighing almost

Mrs Evan Hunter with Ch. Fodhla Patrick 1916.

12 stone (165lb). Many large offers were made to Mrs Hunter to purchase this lovely hound Mrs Hunter always promptly refused. She described him as "beyond price" and declared he was "Her favourite and her constant and devoted companion".

Mrs Hunter then disappears from the wolfhound world and indeed the dog world after making the above statements in December 1916.

It was thought actually, that Captain Hunter had died in his service to the war, but no, he survived. He ended the war in 1918 as a Staff Captain at the War Office and was mentioned in dispatches and was awarded an OBE.

After the war Captain Hunter returned to the law , but sports were his true interest, making athletics his full time career. Eventually becoming Secretary of the British Olympic Association and travelling world wide. Further service in World War II earned him a CBE in 1949.

As for Mrs Hunter, lady of such wolfhound aspirations, there is but one more mention in the archives. Mrs Evan Hunter managed to get to the Ladies singles Championships in Badminton, at the East of Scotland Championships on Tuesday 4th January 1921.

Captain Hunter is mentioned attending Hunt Balls and other occasions, but alone from 1923 onwards.

I can only conclude that Mrs. Evan Hunter died between 1921 and 1923 but sadly I cannot find any further record of the lady that could have and wanted to do so much for the wolfhounds.

Lady Joyce de Malahide portrait 1924 by Bassano.

7 Lady Joyce Talbot de Malahide

IT WAS SOME YEARS AGO that I heard the name Malahide and then discovered that a castle of that name existed. Nowhere though, was there a mention of Irish Wolfhounds, no where at all. After months of sleuthing and some very kind help: here is my story:

James Boswell Talbot, who was to become the 6th Baron Talbot de Malahide, was born 18th March 1874. He was born into the family that had resided at Malahide Castle, near Dublin for nearly 800 years. It was in the early 1920s that James first saw his future wife in a play with a young Noel Coward in Dublin. Joyce Gunning Kerr was from Tickencote, Rutlandshire, in England. The future Lady Talbot took some pursuing, but they eventually married in 1924. As now, Lady Joyce Talbot de Malahide, she received a wonderful welcome to her new home, Malahide Castle. She gave up the stage and settled into the Irish lifestyle. Talbot's great love was horse racing, in which he was able to indulge, as about this time, the family sold some letters belonging to their ancestor, James Boswell the eminent biographer of the 18th Century. James was also interested in fishing and cattle, possessing some wonderful prize winning Jersey Cows.

Around 1925, soon after their marriage, Lady Talbot acquired her first Irish Wolfhound from Isaac W. Everett's Irish wolfhound kennel. Felixstowe Shournagh was born 15th June 1923, being the product of the mating between Felixstowe Kilshane and Felixstowe Kilbernie. Kilshane also sired such famous hounds as Champion Lady of Raikeshill, Champion Clodagh of Ouborough, and Champion Defiane of Grevel.

In 1926 Flexstowe Shournagh was mated to Garda Cormaich whose dam was Garryricken (born 17th March 1917 and sire was Cormac Boroimbe (born 10th March 1917). On the 18th June 1926 Lady Talbot had her first litter, giving this litter the affix "Malahide" to their names: Cathal, Shiela, Shawn, Margarite, Finn and Feardorca.

Lady Talbot did her research well and obviously met and spoke to others in the breed and educated herself as much as possible. In

Malahide Castle

Felixstowe Kilbernie

Felixstowe Shournagh

fact, she must also have been respected by these others in our wolfhound breed, because, although so very new to wolfhounds, she actually partakes in a discussion in a magazine of the day *Cara Na Dilse*, in their September 1928 issue, she states:

"My views on the breed were founded on Mr. Baily's teaching, and I must add that I have found nothing in the library or museum that has made me question his teaching. It seems to me that since Mr. Baily is acknowledged to be a great authority (even Mr. Heaslip volunteers as much), it is a great pity we do not all listen to what he has to tell us. There are many people interested in the breed who are so busy arguing with Mr. Baily that they have not the time left to learn from him. His article in the October IKC (Irish Kennel Club) Journal seems lucid enough. He tells us the breed appears to have died out, but that we can breed dogs very like it. He also warns us that most breeders are, in his opinion, going the wrong way to work".

"Has there ever been a more obvious case of a house divided against itself? If we are trying to revive the Irish Greyhound, we cannot afford to ignore all that Mr. Baily can teach us. I think it can only be those breeders who are governed by purely commercial motives with no feeling for the history of the breed, who persist in placing before the public huge nondescript dogs with various coats and elephantine ears. The clubs have laid down the standard. The breed should be like large deer hounds, but less massive than a Great Dane. And yet Wolfhounds are shown, and even win, which

Lady Talbot de Malahide with her mother and possibly Cathal of Malahide.

far from being less massive than Great Danes, are hardly less massive than prize Highland cattle."

"If I have expressed myself too strongly, may I beg forgiveness from my critics on the grounds that I am sincere and the matter is very near to my heart. My interests are sentimental rather than commercial. I was very pleased when Mr. Baily acclaimed my dog Cathal as the best Irish Wolfhound he ever saw bred in Ireland, but I stand to gain nothing material if the majority of judges agreed with him. I no longer breed the dogs and Cathal is not fit enough for stud, I am sorry to say. He has full brothers available, and I would like to see them appreciated; but if Wolfhound breeders do not want type, so be it. Woman-like, I shall have the last word all to myself, for sentiment having survived, I shall eventually erect a little stone to Cathal, on which I shall say:

"Cathal of Malahide, An Irish Greyhound".

It must be remembered that Mr. John F. Baily was one of the most eminent breeders of the day had been for many years, and was a contemporary of Captain Graham, Crisp, Garnier et al.

Cathal de Malahide was, I think Lady Talbot's favourite hound. What we call our "heart hound" today. I am sincerely hoping that this is a photo of him (see family photos). Sadly Cathal was never bred, and the only hound of her first litter to breed appears to be Margarite, who became an Irish Champion and was owned by Captain R.A.V.Hamilton.

In 1927 Shournagh was bred again, to Chulainn Hannibal, who ws born 12th March 1926. This time there were five in the litter: Brian of Leixlip, Tavoy Michael, Patrick of Malahide, Naidia and Michael of Malahide. These two litters from Shournagh seem to be the only litters that Lady Talbot bred. There are no further records of her involvement with breed later than 1928.

As I state, there are no actual records of Lady Talbot and her wolfhounds, but have I been told that she did attend the Irish Wolfhound Club of Ireland meetings right up until 1950. But, what I do have are memories.

I boldly wrote to the Honourable Rose Talbot de Malahide, who lived in Tasmania. This lady was Lady Talbot's cousin in law, sister to Lord Milo Talbot, the 7th Lord Talbot de Malahide.

Michael of Malahide.

With their prize-winning Irish Wolfhounds: Lord and Lady Talbot de Malahide at the Bray Annual Dog Show late 1920s.

The Honourable Rose Talbot kindly replied to my letter, saying that Lady Talbot was very "keen" on her wolfhounds and that she (Rose) particularly recollects Shournagh around the castle. Lord and Lady Talbot did not have children but liked them and had several god children. I was put in touch with one of her godsons: John. This gentleman did not remember the wolfhounds, but he did recall the peacocks, and how he got into trouble for bringing the feathers into the drawing room. But, as his wife explained, John was young at the time having been born in 1928. It was suggested that I speak to another godson.

This second godson spoke of the late 1920s/ early 1930s, of another world, of how from a tiny child he was sent first with a nanny and then a governess to spend summers at Malahide Castle. "Oh yes" he recalls "the wolfhounds were always around" They used to knock over the china teacups with their tails, and it always caused such a fuss!". I am much indebted to this gentleman, as he sent me some of the photographs included in this chapter.

Lord James Talbot died in 1948, and Lady Talbot remarried a few years later, losing her title. But,

Lady Talbot de Malahide at home with her hounds

The Malahide trophy, photograph by Tim Finney.

on the death of her second husband, she regained it. She returned to England and at the end of her life moved to a nursing home in Sussex, a home that would accept a little dog. Lady Joyce Talbot died in 1980 at the age of 83, with her beloved Yorkshire terrier beside her.

It would seem that I have written about a wealthy lady that had "Irish Wolfhounds" as a hobby. I don't believe that. I think Lady Talbot was passionate about her wolfhounds but severely disappointed. Of the two litters she bred, the only puppies that bred on were sold or given to other people. The puppies she kept died or did not breed.

Her lasting legacy and proof she felt deeply about Irish Wolfhounds is in her gift of the beautiful silver trophy that she donated in 1927 to Irish Wolfhound Club of Ireland. This trophy is in use to this very day, and our present top breeders are proud to win the title "Best in Breed" and have their names added to the roll call on the trophy.

The first winner of this trophy? – well that was Sulhamstead Thelma owned by Florence Nagle. Could we ask for a better recommendation?

Portrait of Isabelle Bruce Reid circa 1934

8 Isabelle Bruce Reid GVMC

THE NAME ISABELLE BRUCE REID sometimes causes confusion in that Bruce Reid has been taken as a man's name or that Bruce Reid was her husband, her name was Isabelle Bruce Reid, called Belle by friends and family. She was born in 1883, the youngest of ten children of Robert Joseph Reid and Mary Jane, nee Clancy. Robert Joseph Reid was a successful textile merchant who had emigrated from Scotland to Victoria, Australia, as a child in 1855. The family lived on a large property in Balwyn. Belle was educated at Genazzano Convent school in Kew. She did well academically, became an accomplished needlewoman, and showed potential as a soprano. She also had a passionate interest in animals particularly horses. Although, Belle wanted to continue to study singing, her parents did not think it suitable for her, coming from an establishment family, to have a career on the stage. Unusually though, they did support her decision to enter the Melbourne Veterinary College, in Fitzroy in 1902.

Graduating in 1906, Belle was the only one of the five final year students to pass the examination. "Belle" (Isabelle) Bruce

Reid GMVC was the first and only woman to qualify from the Melbourne Veterinary College established by William Tyson Kendall in January 1888 following the passing of the Veterinary Surgeons Act of Victoria in December 1887. The course at the Melbourne Veterinary College was given over four years and the final examinations were conducted by the Veterinary Surgeons Board of Victoria. The minutes of the Board Meeting of 28 November 1906 record the results for the 4th year class, and the motion:

"Mr Beckwith moved that Miss Belle Reid be passed the 4th year Examination with 2nd class honours and that she be registered as a Vet Surgeon on payment of the usual fees. Sec. Mr Leitch, and agreed to. "

It is claimed that she became the first female veterinary surgeon in the world, but certainly she was the first in the British Empire.

Belle set up practice near here family home on Whitehorse Road in a house that had formerly accommodated her family's chauffeur. Driving to her calls in a pony and trap, she was a familiar sight in Balwyn.

In 1911 Belle and her sister Mary bought one thousand acres of farmland at Bundoora and names it Blossom Park, (now built up suburbia). In 1923 Belle retired although only 40, and the practice was taken over by Phillip Thomas Kelynack. In 1924 Belle's favourite niece Sylvia Bates married Phillip Thomas Kelynack and he continued to run the veterinary practice until 1967. In 1925 Belle moved to the farm at Blossom Park where she imported an Irish cob stallion, Hafron Sensation, and he provided the main bloodline of her stud.

She also bred Jersey cattle; their names all beginning with Jubilee. Up to this time, Belle had kept pomerannian dogs, I have no idea what began her interest in Irish wolfhounds. She may have made a trip to England between 1923 and 1925. Irish Wolfhounds of a sort were in Australia and New Zealand, mainly mixed with mastiffs or deerhounds for hunting purposes. No Irish wolfhounds were registered at all at this time. It should also be mentioned that from the end of World War One in 1918 until 1923, the Australian government banned all imports of any breed of dog due to fears of rabies which had cropped up in Europe after the war. So perhaps Belle had an earlier interest in wolfhounds but was unable to obtain one.

Whether Belle actually made the trip to England or she corresponded by mail, she got in touch with Captain T H Hudson of the very famous "Brabyns" Irish wolfhound kennels. Sometime in late 1925 three Irish Wolfhounds stepped off a boat in Melbourne: Culleen of Brabyns (Comerford Mick x Hindhead Tarena) born September 8th 1923 and the oldest, Towtas of Brabyns (Ferny of Ifold x Kathleen NaHoulan) born August 4th 1924 and Roscran of Brabyns (Speenham Wolf x Blachnail of Brabys) born June 6th 1925.

These three hounds were the first "official" wolfhounds in Australia, although, only Roscrana and Towtas were actually registered. Belle's first litter was whelped 28th December 1926, Culleen of Brabyns being the dam and Towtas the sire, and they produced 3 dogs: Bruce went to Belle's sister Mary Reid in Canterbury, Finn, who went to a Mrs. H. Stewart in Stonegatta and Tiger to a Miss N. Cook, also of Canterbury. These 3 dogs were all "of Kildare" as their kennel affix. The second litter were also three dogs, Roscrana being the dam and Towtas, naturally, the sire, Leopard and Panther staying at Kildare and Cheetah going to a Mr. L. B. Collins of Brighton, whelped on 12th August 1927. The following year the breeding was repeated between Towtas and Roscrana and on 12th September 1928 a singleton dog Happy Warrior was whelped. Happy Warrior was at first sold to a Mrs. Kinnear of Brighton at five months, but for some reason Happy Warrior was brought back to Kildare and Belle in August of 1929. Happy Warrior seemingly became a huge favourite, as it is he that appears in the only surviving photographs.

First Aussie hound.

Isabelle Bruce Reid in her pony and trap driving to her veterinary calls.

In 1930 Belle imported two more Irish Wolfhounds from Captain Hudson of Brabyns, a dog whelped 21st October 1928 and Lady Myra of Brabyns whelped 28th January 1929. Again I am not sure whether Belle made the long sea voyage to the UK or corresponded to arrange the purchase.

Towtas was bred again the dam does not appear in the records, this time a dog and a bitch puppy Shadow and Sheelah. Sheelah being the first bitch puppy that Belle had bred. Shadow and Lady Myra were mated, which again resulted in a singleton puppy, a dog Malachi, whelped 20th July 1931. Such small litters Belle seems to have had.

This was the last litter under the Kildare prefix, making 5 in total, because inexplicably Belle changed the Kennel affix to Killara.

Happy Warrior of Kildare was bred to Lady Myra of Brabyns and the litter was whelped 22nd November 1932. The three dogs and one bitch were the first litter with the affix Killara, the one bitch Brinda and one dog Garran staying with Belle. Sheelah of Killara (formerly of Kildare) was next bred to Happy Warrior, whelping 1st April 1922, again just two dogs; Tarzan staying at Killara and Thunder going to Mr. Munro of Melbourne.

Sylvia Kelynack and Happy Warrior

Another of Sylvia and Happy Warrior

Happy Warrior accompanying Isabelle Bruce Reid.

Miss Hilda Lascelles with Winlaton Labradors

It is difficult to know when Belle met Hilda Lascelles, perhaps they always knew each other, both coming from establishment families and from the same area. Hilda being some years younger though. Hilda Lascelles was one of the first people in Australia to import Labrador Retrievers. To quote Mary Dalgarno " It is to Miss Lascelles that the credit must go for the main promotion and establishment of the Labrador in Australia." She had acquired her first Labrador in 1930 from Mr. & Mrs Austin's first litter in 1930, the Austins' being the very first to import this breed. Sadly, Eilyer Samson died of distemper after his first show. In late 1933 or early 1934 Belle did actually make the long voyage to the UK. It would be interesting to know whom she visited apart from Captain Hudson at his Brabyn's kennels. She did join the Irish Wolfhound Club and her name can be seen in the membership lists in the later year books. She returned to Australia with a puppy dog Slainge of Brabyns whelped 26th October 1933. For Miss Lascelles she brought two black Labradors, a dog and a bitch which were to be the foundation of Miss Lascelles' famous Winlaton Labrador kennel.

Under the Killara affix there were to be 14 litters altogether, the litters continue to be small, the largest being just 4. Many of the hounds stayed with Belle at her home in Blossom Park, some dogs going to others, but ALL of the bitches stayed with her.

There is little known about the owners, apart from a few names, of the Killara dogs. But one proud owner Mr. Ronald K. Monro who purchased Thunder of Killara, as previously mentioned, wrote a very interesting article in the Irish Wolfhound Club 1937 magazine. As are many Australians, particularly in this era, Mr. Monro was a keen huntsman. To relax away from his job as a newspaper man he loved to go into the bush to hunt Kangaroo, deer and wallabies. Thunder became an admirable hunter and companion to Mr. Munro.

Quoting Mr. Munro, "I can honestly say that he is a really wonderful pal, always by my side ready for a game of serious hunting or a quiet rest. He is a thorough gentleman both at home and abroad, and above all a brilliant and natural hunter."

Hunting was a huge pastime in Australia and many dogs were bred for the hunt, Deer

Thunder of Killara with a fine Sambha Stag he pulled down and Thunder at 8 months of age.

hounds were particularly prized for their speed and stamina. There was a great deal of cross-breeding by some of the hunters to gain size, particularly using the Mastiff, and there was a hound mixture called the Kangaroo Dog, used as is self-explanatory in hunting kangaroos and other fast game. In those days it was not considered improper to cross breed dogs. In fact, in the 1930s Irish Wolfhound Club books, a list of registered cross bred wolfhounds is often given. I think though, Belle did NOT want her precious pure bred wolfhounds cross bred with anything, and that is why she kept all of her bitches and many of her dogs .

Belle's last imported Irish wolfhound was Ninghea of Brabyns whelped 4th March 1936. This bitch was bred by Mrs. Alan Stoddart, not Captain Hudson.

With the help of her niece Sylvia, Belle managed her Blossom Park, right up until her death. She died on 13th December 1945 of coronary thrombosis and was buried in Box Hill cemetery. Her estate was sworn for probate in Australia $101,603. It seems that now Miss Hilda Lascelles stepped in for the hounds, as there were several still remaining at Blossom Park.

Despite her well known love of, and fame in the world of Labradors, Miss Hilda Lascelles has not been mentioned in connection with wolfhounds. She apparently did not mention it herself. Yet it appears that two years before Belle's death, Miss Lascelles took possession of a bitch Kittyhawk and a dog Wirraway. Under her affix Winlaton she actually bred a litter with Kingsford of Killara and Kittyhawk of Killara, producing two dogs and two bitches, they were whelped 3rd August 1947.

In early 1946 soon after Belle's demise she may have felt overwhelmed with dogs, as the records show that Miss Lascelles leased three Irish wolfhounds to Mr. Charles A Venables. Charles Venables was a very well known Deer hound breeder of this time and for next several decades. He was a very notable hunter and bred many different breeds including Borzoi and Labradors. He admitted to crossing to get the size, stamina or speed in his working dogs in order to improve the hunt. Apparently, in 1941 he had imported an Irish wolfhound from New Zealand, possibly to put size to his Deerhounds, there is no proof of that, even though he certainly had some rather large Deerhounds. It seems that Miss Lascelles changed her mind about the leasing of the wolfhounds to Charles Venables. Within just a few months she cancelled the leases and had the hounds returned to her. She never again sold or leased any bitch again, Labrador or Wolfhound.

Charles A Venables

One of Venables large deer hounds.

Miss Hilda Lascelles died in her eighties in the 1980s with a legacy of wonderful Winlaton Labradors in her wake. The Brabyns/Killara line of Irish Wolfhounds and the first registered wolfhounds faded away in the 1950s in Australia. It seems the Irish Wolfhound did not become popular until the early 1970s with new imports.

Isabelle Bruce Reid was almost forgotten until 1996 when her name was included in the National Pioneer Women's Hall of Fame in Alice Spring Northern Territory. Also, in 1996, to celebrate the centenary of Bell's graduation and the contributions made by female veterinarians to the veterinary profession, the University of Melbourne Faculty of Veterinary Science established the Belle Bruce Reid Honour Roll on the 28th November 2006.

100 female veterinarians are named on this roll and include women who graduated overseas and made their contributions in Australia and women who graduated from schools in Australia and made their contributions elsewhere in the world.

Portrait of Rudolph Valentino.

9 Rudolph Valentino

I THINK MOST OF US HAVE HEARD OF RUDOLPH VALENTINO – the heart throb of the film world in the early 1920s. Born in Italy in 1895, he went to the United states in 1913, where due to his lack of English he became a dancer. In 1918 he had work as a "film extra". However, by 1922, due to his smouldering good looks, and at the age of 27, he was the top box office "leading man" of the movie world, celebrated and adored.

In 1924 he bought a huge mansion in Berverly Hills, his first and only real home of his own. "Falcon Lair" was an estate of 8 acres where Valentino could indulge in his passion for horses and dogs and retreat from public life.

Along with the Arabian horses, Valentino owned several dogs, including three Great Danes, but his favourites were a Doberman named Kabal and his beloved Irish Wolfhound Centaur Pendragon. Centaur Pendragon as the name implies, came from Mrs Glen Stewart and her then new Irish Wolfhound Centaur Kennels in Maryland.

Sinn Feinn & Puppies with Mrs. Stewart owner of the Centaur Kennels.

Valentino's home "Falcon Lair"

Bally Shannon

Valentino with his horse and Centaur Pendragon.

Valentino at home with his Great Dane and Centaur Pendragon

Pendragon in the movie "Son of the Sheik" in 1926, Valentino's final movie.

Centaur Pendragon's sire was Champion Bally Shannon, born October 14th 1919, then owned by Reverend Hildebrand of Essex, England. Bally Shannon went to Mrs. Stewart in 1921, and it was said that he became her favourite hound of all time. He was mated to Sinn Fein, born 2nd June 1921, who was bred by Ralph Montague Scott. Centaur Pendragon was whelped 4th December 1924, one of 14 puppies, surprisingly for those days, all survived and I believe it was Mrs. Stewart's first litter.

Pendragon was Valentino's constant companion and usually travelled with him, his job was to guard his master's luggage, all 79 pieces of it. The wolfhound also appeared in the movie *The Sheik* with Valentino.

Sadly, Valentino did not have long to enjoy his fame and wealth or his lovely home and dogs. He died in 1926, aged just 31, from septicaemia from a perforated ulcer, no antibiotics then. A rather ghastly death.

Valentino with Pendragon off travelling on the train.

Interestedly after his demise, it was discovered that Valentino was actually hugely in debt, up to a million dollars. His friends organised an auction of his belongings, printing an "Estate Catalogue", a book that is highly collectible today. Along with the house, auto mobiles and the Arabian horses are the dogs.

I wonder what happened to Centaur Pendragon and the other dogs? I like to think he was returned to Mrs Stewart at Centaur Kennels.

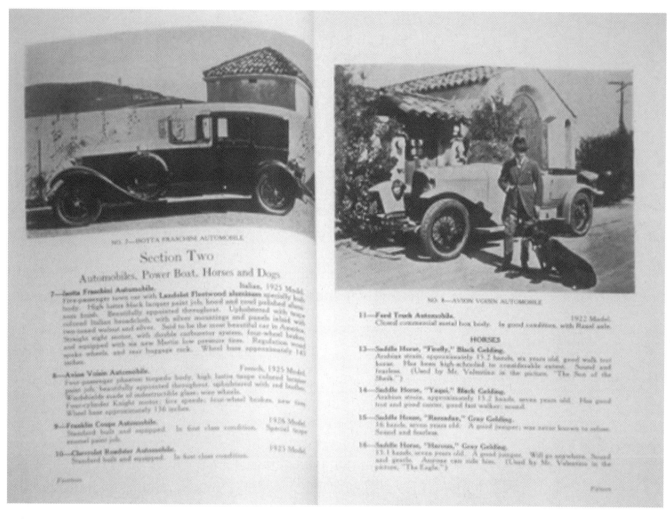

Valentino's Estate Catalogue.

Another of Douglass Montgomery and Gaelic King.

Padraic of Ambleside was born March 5th, 1933 another wheaten boy. The sire was Sulhamstead Dan of Ambleside and his dam was Top Lady of Ambleside, both came from Alma Starbuck's famous kennels, Ambleside in Michigan.

It was around this time that Douglass and his parents moved to an estate situated in the country between Atadena and Pasadena, still in California. Their beautiful estate was in the area known as Edgecliffe. A neighbour in this area was a Mr. Thomas Wanamaker and it was Douglass who introduced Thomas Wanamaker to Irish Wolfhounds but that is another story, although Thomas Wanamaker was to figure in Douglass' life. The photo is of Padraic with one of Thomas' dachshunds.

Padraic was Douglass' constant companion and went to all the restaurants and nightclubs that Douglass visited, Douglass often with a lady on his arm. Local newspapers of the time commented on the affectionate nature of the actor's large friend and how both were welcomed everywhere.

In 1934 Douglass starred in a film titled *Little Man What Now?*. The film was about a small man in a big world confronting middle class problems. His performance was considered to be the best of the year by many, but criticised by others, as they disbelieved that a "young man born in the lap of luxury could truly play the part of the underdog".

Padraic was on the set set at Universal studios everyday while

Padraic of Ambleside with Wannamakers dachshund.

Douglass was filming for this part. A newspaper at that time published the photo with the caption: "A Little Man and Big Dog", obviously referring to the film.

Douglass was truly a "companion" owner, he didn't ever breed. Actually, I don't think he even joined the Irish Wolfhound Club of America until after World War II. It was his interest and his love of having a hound beside him, that made him continue with our breed. Certainly there is no mention of him even attending shows until much later.

When Padraic died Douglass was heartbroken, and yet again it was reported in the Pasadena and Hollywood newspapers – I feel Douglass found the newspapers' reportage rather intrusive at times.

Douglass continued to base his home at Edgecliffe, Pasadena, where his good friend Thomas B. Wanamaker was continuing with his own involvement with wolfhounds. Douglass leaving for for his acting commitments, including *Mystery of Edwin Drood*, for which he won some acclaim.

1934 article about Douglass in the film *Little Man What Now*.

Montgomery with Isolde "he is in a courting mood" said a Newspaper of the day.

In the middle of 1937 Douglass once again visited Alma Starbuck at her Ambleside Kennels. This time he acquired his first bitch. Isolde of Ambleside who was born April 2nd 1937, again a wheaten hound. The photograph of Douglass on the phone with a hound, I feel sure is her as Douglass looks more mature and somehow the hound looks like a girl. This is another newspaper photograph with the caption: "Douglass Montgomery calling Wendy Barrie. He's in a courting mood"!

There is little information about Isolde as the world's attention was focused on the coming war. She did stay safely with Thomas B. Wanamaker at the Edgecliffe kennels while Douglass was away. Alma Starbuck was to comment some years later that "Isolde of Ambleside lived to a ripe old age".

In 1940 Douglass joined the Canadian Infantry and went to Europe. He was though, soon demobilised in order to appear in a film *The Way to the Stars*, a film made to cement Anglo-American relations. Douglass considered this his best performance.

Staying on in England Douglass went on to direct and also appear in television productions, he also though, returned often to his Pasadena home. In the late 1940s Douglass met Kathleen Tamor Young. She was described as "London born and Paris educated", she was an actress and costume designer.

Although, Douglass lived in London most of the time in the 1940s he was not without a beloved wolfhound. This hound was another male; Hound of Heaven. Further background information on Hound of Heaven was impossible to find, as he was not registered to Douglass, remembering that Douglass was always a companion owner, but it has been suggested that he was from the Grevel Kennels.

Hev, as he was affectionately called, did have an interesting escapade with Royalty.

"One day some years ago", recounted the actor; "our housekeeper was taking Hev for his daily walk through a London park. She was a prim middle aged woman who loved Hev but had a hard time handling the big hound.

When about midway in the park, on this particular day, she was approached by an uniformed man who ask if she would step over to a car at the curb. The housekeeper was indignant at being accosted by a stranger, but because of his insistence complied. Hev, like so many Irish Wolfhounds, just loved to ride in cars, and when he saw the door of this one open, he jumped in, leaving the housekeeper aghast, for she recognised the occupant of the back seat, as the Queen Mother Mary.

BEST MOVER—Ch. Tralee of Cu—owned by Mrs. Graham was best moving I.W. At left is Mrs. John W. Wofford, donor of the challenge trophy; right is Mrs. Douglass Montgomery, donor of "keep" award in memory of her late husband.

Mrs Douglass Montgomery on the right of the photo.

Between the housekeeper and the chauffeur, Hev was finally extricated from the limousine, but not before the Queen Mother had admired and petted him and asked innumerable questions, including the inevitable "What kind of dog is he?"

"It was a big event in the life of our housekeeper, and she never tires of telling the story over and over". Hound of Heaven died quietly of good age at Christmas 1950.

In the middle of the year of 1950 Douglass made another of his frequent trips home to the United States, but this time taking with him Kinsale of Boroughbury, a three year bitch in whelp, that Thomas B. Wanamaker had purchased from Mrs. Allnett of Kinsale.

The Westminster dog show of 1951 is the first show on record that Douglass attended along with his good friend Thomas B. Wanamaker, both as observers. It was also 1951 that saw his permanent return to his family home in Pasadena. In 1952 he married Kathleen Tamor Young at the home of his friends Governor and Mrs. John D. Lodge, at the Governor's House in Hartford, Connecticut. They returned from Hartford to live in Douglass' home in Pasadena.

Douglass' last stage appearance was in the *Legend of Lizzie* which opened in the worst snow storm in years and the show closed soon after.

He decided to retire from acting and he and Kathleen and Thomas B. Wanamaker moved to Eagle Rock, Darien, Connecticut. There the three of them opened a shop "KYM" (Kathleen Young

Montgomery), a made to order for dresses establishment, Kathleen being the designer. The business achieved overnight success and had to be expanded.

At Eagle Rock in Darien, Thomas resuscitated his Edgecliffe kennels with Douglass in attendance. There is even some mention of Douglass actually handling in the show ring. His interest in the show ring though, was minimal compared to his interest in the actual hounds.

There is an account of Douglass asking a friend at the 1965 Irish Wolfhound Speciality for the correct way of congratulating the handler Jim Scanlon on Edgecliffe Timothy winning RWD (Reserve Winners Dog). Truly, a kind and courteous man.

A more revealing account of this companion of the past took place shortly before his death. He was staying as a guest where half a dozen wolfhounds shared the host's bedroom. At 5 am the hounds demanded to be let out and clattered downstairs in a great rush. The racket woke Douglass who remarked that he could not think of a better way to be awakened, and that he enjoyed the noise the wolfhounds made.

Sadly, Douglass became ill in early 1966, he was diagnosed with cancer of the spine and died in July 1966 aged just 59; a gentleman and a true friend to our breed.

The last photograph is probably my favourite as it really shows how much love Douglass had for his companions.

A wonderful photograph of Montgomery with Padraic.

William J. Dammarell in the 1950s.

11 William J. Dammarell

WHEN I WAS FIRST ASKED ABOUT WILLIAM J. DAMMARELL I must admit my mind drew a blank, until I was reminded of the following poem of which William J. Dammarell was the author:

Death of a Hound

The great Heart cracks; the mighty frame
In chill of death has turned to stone
With silence in the empty halls
We sit alone.

Too numb to weep, too desolate
For tears or pain-releasing sight.
A puppy stumbles up to us –
Kings do not die!

I am sure this short but poignant poem is familiar to many of us. Thus it became my pleasure to find out more about this gentleman. Naturally, this had some difficulties as I live in the Scottish Borders and William J. Dammarell lived in Cincinnati, Ohio in the United States, and there was lamentably very little information on the world wide web for this poet of ours.

So I tackled my problem the old fashioned way with a telephone and telephone directory. Many fruitless phone calls later I was at last introduced to the very charming family of William J. Dammarell. It was through a grandson and his wife that I was put in touch with two daughters, Anne at first, and then Mary, both remembered their parents poetry and their wolfhounds so well.

Mary, very kindly, shared with me her family and personal wolfhound memories, which I quote in full:

The Family Hounds

"Ten Irish Wolfhounds grew up in the Dammarell nursery, Bill and Elizabeth had moved their children into Oakwood some years before Bill fulfilled a childhood dream and bought one of the legendary hounds. At six months, Brian Boru was rangy, brindled and not fully grown but at least 36 inches at the shoulder.

One of the little girls was afraid of dogs, Ann had been assured she would love the baby animal. The newly arrived and frisky Brian was presented to her at naptime. The tiny tyke looked up at the huge face and cried,

The Dammarell Family

"that's not a puppy. That's a 'normous dog!' . Another problem existed. There was a cat in residence. Cat and puppy hissed, chased and behaved with great animosity. Then Elizabeth sat down in the library with the cat – back arched and claws unsheathed – in one arm and Brian's great head held firmly on her lap. She repeatedly explained to them that she understood their opposing natures but they were both part of the family and had to behave. The children thought this incident was proof their mother was mad. The animals understood her. They never became curled up together friends but from that time on they ceased being enemies.

The five children quickly made Brian a member of the family and the next year Andrea, Andy, was introduced. She was darker, smaller and amazingly aloof for an Irish Wolfhound. Bill had craftily given her as a gift to Elizabeth on whom responsibility for the care and feeding of both children and dogs rested. They bonded immediately.

Despite the fact that Brian had contracted a disease which left him with a noticeable tremor, he had grown and prospered. It is possible a doctor friend saved Brian by injecting him with a new experimental medicine said to have served well on the battlefront. It was penicillin. The result of two young healthy dogs roaming the halls was predictable. They met and courted in Elizabeth's mother's bedroom before her horrified Edwardian eyes.

Oakwood is one of those castle-like homes beloved in both the British Isles and America by wealthy Victorian merchants. It came complete with a tower, underground passages and a chapel wing. In the 1940s the wing's first floor was devoted to the kitchen and laundry and the second floor had servants quarters and a nursery with a very large bathroom. The bathroom had a lion clawed cast iron tub and a great expanse of marble flooring. It was deemed a perfect birthing chamber for puppies.

At the time the puppies were born, William John Dammarell, a successful trial lawyer, was the Federal District Attorney for the Southern District of Ohio. He would later be appointed Common Pleas Judge. Oakwood, his home then became known ever after, not as the Dammarell's or even the Castle. It was "The House with the BIG DOGS".

The eagerly anticipated birth occurred while the family was at noon Mass. When the older children reported the presence of tiny, wet, furry creatures, the veterinary was called. By the time he arrived, Andy had easily produced nine little puppies and licked them into breathing. Mary could not believe such a big dog would have such small offspring. She thought they looked like mice. The final pup Andy ignored and the vet took over. This smallest one, the runt, would grow up to be the big blond much loved Jimmy

The puppies

who lived his whole life with the Dammarells as Michael's dog. He was named after a small blond boy who belonged to a ballroom dance class attended by the older children. Mercifully the adolescent never made the connection.

World War Two had ended over a year before but there was still meat rationing in the US. So the family ate out and used their ration cards for the dogs. A cousin of Elizabeth's had a friend with a farm and brought in goat's milk to supplement Andy's nursing. The kitchen reeked of goat's milk and something supposed to be nourishing. It could have been cod liver oil. The little babies needed bottles every few hours during the first days. The whole family took turns holding a skinny puppy upside down in one hand and a bottle in the other. As a little dog sucked its belly would begin to grow round. Then it would lie on its back with its legs in the air and grow right before the feeder's eyes. The blind "mice" were as big as Cocker Spaniels in six weeks and growing fast.

They stayed in the house most of the time. In the early days, Andy would circle the bathroom checking on them all. If she became agitated it meant one of the puppies had crawled under the tub and had to be pulled out. Eventually they moved into the unused nursery. When they were a little older the dogs were taken out. As the nursery door opened, the puppies raced past the hand carved banisters – first to the landing then to the main hall. It looked like a wave of bright multicoloured fur and it sounded like thunder and strange clicking as their paws hit the broad wooden stairs.

It was understood by the Dammarells that many European Irish Wolfhounds had to be put down because of food shortages during the war. Kennels were sometimes lucky to keep one breeding pair. It was said that there were only about one hundred Irish Wolfhounds in the world at that time – and ten of them were in the nursery at Oakwood. The official home name selected for the puppies was Clontarf Kennel in honour of Brian Boru's victory over the Danes in 1013. Each puppy was given an official name beginning with C.

The puppies grew and were taught some of Brian's old tricks. The oldest daughter had just started high school and in the coming years some of the young men who came to see Mary were not overjoyed to be met by a friendly dog who easily put its paws on their shoulders and looked down to lick an unsuspecting face.

Clearly all the puppies could not stay. They were very much in demand and one by one many were shipped away – sold or as gifts. Jimmy and Casear, the largest of the litter who measured 39 inches at the shoulder, remained the longest. They considered themselves people or at the very least lap dogs.

Jimmy and Caesar with Judge Dammarell Enquirer 1950

The family did not care for showing the dogs. They felt it was very hard on the hounds. Occasionally, Jimmy or Casear would go with a friend who wanted to show his Irish Wolfhound and needed some other of the breed for competition. The Dammarell hounds would not be carefully groomed to help the show dog. Sometimes this worked. Sometimes it did not and the Clontarf Kennel entry won. Once in Alabama, Jimmy escaped and took off into the hills. No one could catch him. People began to talk of sighting a big tawny mountain lion. Hunters got out their guns. There was fear for Jimmy's safety. Michael was sent off by plane – a teen with a mission. As soon as he was brought to the wooded area where the "mountain lion"" was last seen, Michael whistled and his dog came bounding out. Closer to home, the Cincinnati Police came to know when one of the hounds was wandering if they got hysterical calls about wild animals. They would call the judge and an expedition would capture the culprit.

Life was less complex then. People often did not lock their doors. Sometimes callers at Oakwood would hammer the lion knocker to no avail. If they were very foolish, they could then push open the heavy oak door and enter the home. They did not leave. Although the dogs never harmed a human visitor, it was occasionally possible that a family member would return home to find a terrified person cornered in one of the rooms.

The last wolfhound to live with Bill and Elizabeth was Kerry. He was the offspring of one of the puppies and the Dammarells had given him to their friend, the Rev. Karl Alter, Archbishop of Cincinnati as a pup. Kerry roamed the Archbishop's palace and charmed the staff. As he got older, however, he took to leaving the grounds and visiting the canine ladies of the neighbourhood. For the sake of clerical propriety, Kerry returned to Oakwood where he was the huge and patient playmate of the Dammarell's toddler grandchildren. They climbed on his resting back and pulled his fur. Only when the tiny fingers began to poke his eyes would the long suffering hound rise with a sigh. The children would tumble off unharmed without so much as a warning growl to discourage their future advances.

The great fondness Bill and Elizabeth felt for their friends, the hounds, is clear in their poetry.

Elizabeth and grandchild with Kerry 1960

The family in the early 1960s with Kerry

They both loved history, faith, truth, mystery, and strong, living traditions. They created a wonderful world of reflection, inspiration and anticipation for their friends and family. They raised their children in a larger than life atmosphere. The Irish Wolfhounds were part of that experience."

Judge Dammarell loved all things Irish and his Irish ancestry, particularly its legends and poetry, hence the purchase of his first wolfhound Fair Patrick. Fair Patrick, though was always called Brian Boru. Judge Dammarell also loved the law, starting his legal career with the Ohio Dept. of State. He was appointed Federal District Attorney, in Cincinnati shortly after the start of World War 11. He became Judge of Hamilton County Common Pleas Court on March 10th 1950. He continued his private law practise almost until his death. Judge Dammarell was always writing and published many articles and short stories. He was a member of the "Writers League" and the "Canticle Guild", both Cincinnati writing groups. It is, of course, his poetry that has brought so much pleasure to the Irish Wolfhound world. Elizabeth too, wrote poetry:

(first and last verses) Cead Mile Failte:
It's the language of love when you open the door
It's Macushla, Mavouree, Allanah, Astore
It is't a plaint and it isn't a moan
But sure, its the typical Wolfhound tone.

Most poignant sound in the world to hear
Filled to its echo with joy and tear
Heart speaks to Heart on Friendship's ground
In the wordless speech of the Irish hound.

Mary told me that no odd piece of paper or old envelope could be thrown out in case there was some scribbling in preparation for a future poem, on that little scrap.

Fair Patrick was born 29th September 1944 sired by Padraic of Summerhill and dam; Ambleside Fair Fan of Kihone. He came to live with the Dammarells from Alma Starbuck on the Good Friday of 1945. Always called Brian Boru after the lengendary Biran Boru who died in battle on that day in 1013 AD.

Barnhill Andrea joined the family the following Good Friday, by coincidence, in 1946, and always called Andy.

Those ten puppies that were born that December 22nd 1946 were Caitlin, Ceol, Cormac, Caoin-Keen, Cashel, Colan, Conan, Conn, Conor, and Cuisle.

Debbie Dammarell, grand daughter of Judge Dammarell in 1960

All were registered individually with the American Kennel Club in December of 1947.

As Mary states in her "memories", not all the puppies could stay will the Dammarell family. Clontarf Caoin went to Sylvestor O'Toole of the Tuahil affix and was bred twice to Cheevers of Ambleside. Clontarf Ceol went to Alma Starbuck and was bred to Finn-MacCumaill of Ambleside . Clontarf Cormac stayed with the family for longer and was called Tark; but then he went to Kill Kiracher – a most handsome hound who became a US Champion, but was never put to stud. Clontarf Caoin (pronounced Keen), Clontarf Conn, who became Jimmy and Clontarf Conor, who became Caesar all stayed at Oakwood. The remaining four were given as companion gifts to wolfhound friends.

Mr. LeRoy Fess and his wife Margaret were particularly good friends. Mr. Fess being the early long time editor of the Harp and Hound in those 1950s days and the owner of the kennel affix Taraledge. Writing in the American Kennel Gazette of April 1948, Mr. Fess says in admiration of a particular Christmas card, he received from Judge Dammarell; "The card shows an action group sketch in silhouette – a brace of hounds held on leash by a powerful nude male, all standing on the pointing arrow of a weather vane. Action is the dominate tone of the assemblage". Judge Dammarell, in response, explains this lovely sounding Christmas card was actually taken as a copy from his "house number bracket" which was an original done by his friend, Joseph Pfister, an acclaimed artist at this time. A few other recipients of this admired card were Alma Starbuck, Mrs Norwood B. Smith, Charles W. Strohm and Charles D Burrage among others. I wonder if anyone has kept their copy? Andy (Barnhill Andrea) mother of the Clontarf pups, tragically died in 1949, in a car accident. Brian Boru died of a "broken heart" within a few months in early 1950. In the Fall issue of the *Harp & Hound*, Margaret Fess describes a visit, a wonderful visit, to Oakwood and the Dammarells. By then Jimmy and Caesar had also passed on. Mrs. Fess describes their visit to Oakwood in some detail; the 14ft ceilings, the high hanging chandeliers, giving flickering shadows against the panelled walls, the huge house being just the place for King Arthur and his round table. Sadly, at this time no wolfhounds were in residence to add to the atmosphere. To Mrs Fess's delight and enjoyment though, Judge Dammarell arranged for among others, Robert Powell to come for the evening with his wolfhound Melody of Melody Lane. Melody being a Clontarf Jimmy X Rathrahilly Conemara offspring. Mrs. Fess felt that Melody's presence fit the house so well. On that same visit the Fesses were introduced to the Archbishop of Cincinnati; the Most Reverand Karl J. Altar who at that time still owned Tuahil of Sligo, affectionately called Kerry. As Mary has written, the Archbishop had some difficulty with Kerry, in that Kerry had a fondness for escaping the bishop's palace grounds in the search of "ladies", so he returned to the Dammarells and proved to be an enormous favourite with everyone.

Oakwood Manor.

Kerry was the last of the wolfhounds to reside at Oakwood. Elizabeth Dammarell died in 1972 and Judge Dammarell, at 87, in July 1993. Up until the end though, he continued to write articles, short stories and his poetry.

Judge Dammarell and his wife Elizabeth's involvement in the Irish wolfhound world could be said to be mainly as companion owners, as so many of us are, I think all of us in the breed though will be for ever grateful for their beautiful poetry – a legacy that will go on. I do hope they are pleased.

Portrait of Celeste Winans Hutton

12 Celeste Winans Hutton

THERE ARE QUITE A FEW PEOPLE TODAY who had the great pleasure of knowing Celeste Winans Hutton. Even though, it is thirty years since her death, she is still thought of with much fondness and happy memories.

She was well known in the dog world, particularly in her home state of Maryland, but to us in the Irish Wolfhound fancy she was known for her Greysarge Kennels. Living at her home and kennels she devoted her life to her hounds and cairn terriers, but also to an assortment of rescue dogs. It is, perhaps not quite so well known that her family, going back some generations, were part of the "backbone" of the history of America.

Ross Winans was born in 1797 in the state of New Jersey, as a young man he showed extraordinary adeptness for industrial engineering, a new concept in those days. He married Julia DeKay and moved to Baltimore, Maryland, in 1827. Ross Winans, unaware that he was something of a genius in engineering, began to invent techniques to the, then new, locomotive industry and became strongly associated with the innovative company called "the

Baltimore and Ohio Railroad". In a few years, Ross Winans and his two sons William and Thomas were building all the engines for the Baltimore and Ohio Railroad Company. Their success in this new field became known internationally. So well known that Czar Nicholas I of Russia tried to persuade Mr. Winans to assist his country with Russia's new rail road system. Ross Winans refused the offer but sent his sons instead.

Ross Winans also had an interest in sanitation and public welfare, publishing pamphlets and lobbying for the development of a public water supply for the city of Baltimore. He developed low income housing projects, calling them working men's housing. In fact to this day a public housing project in the Baltimore area is called Mount Winans.

Ross Winans 1796 – 1877

William and Thomas Winans did very well in Russia organizing a straight rail road from St Petersburg to Moscow, a feat, French engineers had said was impossible.

Both sons amassed rather large fortunes as a consequence. Thomas while in Russia met and married Celeste Revillion a Russian lady of French and Italian ancestry who had been a lady in waiting to the Tzarina. On their return to America, Thomas built their family home in Baltimore city, "Alexandrofsky House", and their summer home Orianda, on their estate Crimea, also near Baltimore. William eventually settled in Kent in England, and never returned to the United States, having a fear of the ocean, despite having helped design a peculiar ship called "the cigar boat". William's

Thomas Winans

Alexandrofsky House

son Walter owned several large estates in England and Scotland pursuing mainly the breeding and racing of horses. Celeste's family was not without glamour, a sister of Thomas and William; Beatrice, married Prince Henri De Bearn de Chalais. This gentleman actually having had a scandal in his history, namely a duel over the right of his use of the name de Chalais. Also, through the marriage of Ross Winans to Julia de Kay, Celeste was related to the very famous artist Whistler. Many very worthy ancestors were involved with the civil war, or were involved in politics or education. The Winans family in Baltimore were considered one of the first in "society"!

Thomas Winans and Celeste Revillon had a daughter Celeste Marguerite Winans who married Gaun Mc Robert Hutton, an Irishman and diplomat. They in turn had a son Reginald Hutton who married Mabel Dorothea Finn, their daughter was Celeste Winans Hutton.

Celeste Winans Hutton was born June 14th 1923 into a family of wealth, position and part of Baltimore society. Educated at private schools, she went on to Goucher College for her bachelor degree and then a post-graduate degree in Animal Husbandry. Celeste could have gone on to live a life of ease and comfort, but the life of a "Society Princess" would not suit Celeste Hutton at all. She devoted her life to the care and concern for animals.

Celeste joined the Maryland chapter of the "Society for the Prevention of Cruelty to Animals in 1946 at just 23, becoming their Recorder Secretary the following year . She was also one of the founding members of the Maryland Pony Show, continuing her interest and support in that organization for the rest of her life.

In the late 1940s Celeste started breeding and showing Cairn Terriers, also purchasing the property on Falls Road on the outskirts of Baltimore. This property was henceforth known as Greysarge. Her first Irish Wolfhound was Windale Killala, whelped 11th May 1950, but purchased in 1952. It was the further purchase in 1954, of Fuath of Nendrum, that was to bring Celeste great success in the show ring. Fuath was whelped 27th January 1951 and had two previous owners before Celeste. Already, a Champion in Ireland where he was born he became a Champion in both Canada and the United. In those days, Fuath was perhaps the only Champion in three countries simultaneously. Although, Fuath took Best of Breed in Show 63 times, I think this wolfhound captured Celeste heart while as a companion at home at Greysarge.

A newspaper article of the time published an interview with Celeste during 1959 where she explains the pampered life of her dear Fuath, "the largest dog in all of Maryland". Apparently, his plane ticket in 1954 cost $400, a large sum, but Celeste declined to say how much Fuath's purchase price was, "he is priceless to me anyway" she declared. "He will only eat from a chair or table, and flopped so much on the furniture I had everything covered in plastic. The air conditioning was installed for the hounds, not only in the house, where only Fuath is allowed, but also the day

A young Celeste.

Another, of the young Celeste at home.

and night kennels next to the house. Also, Fuath sleeps on my bed with me." Celeste went on to say in this interview. Fuath was her favourite subject, always called Fuath of Ulaid in public, he was called Fumphy Wumphy at home.

It seems the whole property of Greysarge was given over to Celeste's dogs. The kitchen was always covered with many many food bowls, the carpet was taken up in favour of tiles and the afore mentioned air conditioning, still a new and expensive addition in the 1950s. There could be a great many dogs up to 28, at Greysarge, at any one time, not just the cairn terriers and wolfhounds but also several rescue dogs were given a home.

Cragwood Caren and Cristel of Ambleside had joined the Greysarge household in 1952 both were bred from, but not shown much. It was another dog from Ireland that was to bring further success in the showring.

Taraheen Tartan was bred by a interesting person, Mrs Annette O'Flaherty of County Wexford. Mrs O'Flaherty had been the housekeeper to the Gardeners when they moved to Ireland from England. Coolafin wolfhounds were in nearly all of Mrs O'Flaherty's wolfhounds and Tartan's Sire and Dam were both bred from Irish Monarch and Julia of Coolafin. Tartan was whelped 14th April 1954 but did not arrive in America until 1958 already an Irish Champion. He was re-registered with the American Kennel club as Castledawn Tartan that same year. Like Fuath, Tartan became an American Champion.

During the 1950s, Celeste was very active in the show ring, travelling to Canada and as far south as South Carolina, but not in the summer months, too hot for the dogs and for herself. She also had a few litters and Fuath and Tartan were put to stud. She was also very successfully showing her Cairn terriers. Nevertheless she was extremely hard working with the SPCA of Maryland. Along with her rescue dogs, she certainly had a busy life. She joined the Irish Wolfhound Club of America in 1956, and was immediately on various committees. At the same she was a very active member of the Cairn Terrier Club of America and was in fact President for three years of that organization. This alone kept her very busy.

At the close of the 1950s and beginning of the 1960s Celeste still showed but did not breed her wolfhounds although Greysarge MacNamara of Powerscourt was put to stud twice in 1974 and 1975. She always had a few, from her own breeding, or purchased or re homed. Tartan's last litter that he sired was in 1960, to a home bred Greysarge Laurie of Cu. She certainly seemed to favour wolfhounds from Ireland when she purchased hounds. Wolfhounds were always at Greysarge right up until her death.

More significant was her continuing concern for animals and huge involvement with the SPCA of Maryland. She was often asked to be a contributing columnist in such specialised publications as *The Middleburg Chronicle*, (horses) and the *American Kennel Club Gazette*. As had her grandfather 80 years

Celeste in the 1970s

CH. CHRISTEL OF AMBLESIDE

IRISH, AM., and CAN. CH. FUATH OF ULAID

ROSSKEEM OF RIMWOLD

CH. CASTLEDAWN TARTAN

Some of the Greysarge Irish wolfhounds

before, Celeste was elected President of the SPCA of Maryland in 1974. Early in her tenure Celeste protested to the American army about using beagle dogs in their military and medical research. So vigorously did she pursue this, that in 1975 the Military stopped the purchase and use of 450 beagles in their research for the whole of that year. Sadly beagles were used again but in much less quantities.

The beautiful old Mansion Evergreen on the Falls was the headquarters of the SPCA in Maryland and Celeste spent a great deal of time there, she organized the rebuilding of the kennels and cattery. She also converted an old pump house into a lecture room for instruction purposes. Also Celeste started a comprehensive library one of the most generous donors to this was Mrs Florence Nagle, who gave many stud books, magazines and pictures. Celeste wanted to create a haven for animal lovers, where they could research, study and pass on their knowledge.

Celeste was only 57 when she died, in October 1980 from heart disease, (as did her father), at the Union Memorial Hospital in

Celeste in the late 1970s at a dog show.

Evergreen Mansion, headquarters of the Society for the Prevention of Cruelty to Animals.

Baltimore. The Cathedral of Mary Our Queen was filled to the brim at her funeral.

It seems that Celeste is best remembered for her enormous self deprecating wit; she told very amusing stories, her kindness to so many, her great care of her own dogs and her tireless work on behalf of all animals. Most of all though, for her generosity of spirit and her unfailing good sportsmanship and cheerfulness. She left behind very many good close friends and was sorely missed. As one friend said after she died,

"The animals are crying and so are we".

"GREYSARGE", Cockeysville, Maryland

A copy of a personal postcard that Celeste used to send notes.

Celeste's grave

"Baltimore can be proud that one of the oldest organizations to prevent cruelty to animals is in this city. Since 1869 the Maryland SPCA has made its stand so that in the case of the animals – Justice Shall be Done!"

Justice for Animals

"Each individual who takes on the responsibility of care for a living thing must be a true paragon of justice because he is mute and cannot complain through either the spoken or written word. Sometimes the scars are buried deep and cannot be seen until the cruelty is so great that life itself is in jeopardy and trust is gone. When man took upon himself the domestication of animals, he made himself liable for their protection. Among the resulting obligations are:

Plenty of food and water

Good clean, dry shelter

Protection from over breeding and overproducing through law and common sense.

Protection from being overworked.

Proper limitation of activity through fencing and leashing to prevent injury.

A kind word and a kind hand.

Justice is the quality of thought that protects him, who gives and him who receives – animal or man. Animals have their own codes of behaviour which produce equities and procedures (the greatest good for the greatest number) that permit the Animal Kingdom to survive through its own depletion and reproduction. In an informed community it is only just to consider the plight of God's dumb creatures and attempt to better their lot"

CELESTE WINANS HUTTON
President, The Maryland Society for the Prevention of Cruelty to Animals.

Reprinted from the Baltimore Daily Record with permission.

Celeste's car ornament.